Brininstool + Lynch

Brininstool + Lynch

Brininstool + Lynch
Making Architecture
1989–2019

Essay by Reed Kroloff

THE MONACELLI PRESS

Library of Congress Control Number: 2019905062

ISBN 978-1-58093-532-6

10 9 8 7 6 5 4 3 2 1

Printed in China

ANDREA MONFRIED EDITIONS

Design by Steve Liska, Liska + Associates

The Monacelli Press
6 West 18th Street
New York, New York 10011

www.monacellipress.com

Contents

Means and Methods
Brad Lynch

On the second floor of our office is a photograph of an eraser shield by the New York photographer John Back. We often pause in front of this work when we give potential employees a tour of the office. As time passes, fewer people can identify the tool or its purpose.

When David Brininstool and I formed our studio on the near west side of Chicago back in 1989, architects still drafted by hand. The office was quiet, and frequently a technical pen would cut into the Mylar we used for construction drawings, making an unmistakable etching noise. To be efficient with drawing ink on Mylar, you had to have a technique: pulling on the parallel rule slightly so that the ink would not blot, angling the pen a little so that the ink would flow evenly. If the lines of corners intersected and overlapped, the ink would pool to form a rounded corner. It was at this point that the eraser shield came into play. You would go back to the crossed lines with an eraser that was cut at a sharp angle, lightly moisten the edge with your tongue, and use the eraser shield to produce a perfect line and corner. It was a reductive approach to drafting, and it was a process that embodied our approach to architecture.

Every work of architecture begins with a client and a wish list. Rarely does the client—or the designer—get everything on the list. Of his founding gift to the University of Chicago and its ambitious first president, William Harper, John D. Rockefeller said, "I gave him an unlimited budget and he exceeded it." It is in finding the right balance—program to cost, cost to schedule—that the expertise, experience, and judgment of the architect are revealed. We use less of what costs more while still achieving a fresh spatial experience, a play of light and shadow, and a sense of anticipation. We hide what can be hidden and express what is important. We endeavor to capture the meaningful elements of a form and express them simply, reductively.

The same approach is evident in this book. Although we have completed more than 250 projects in our thirty years, here we show only twelve. They vary in size, type, geography, and budget, but they evidence a thread common to all our work: a composition of carefully detailed materials that both observes and evolves the tradition of modernism.

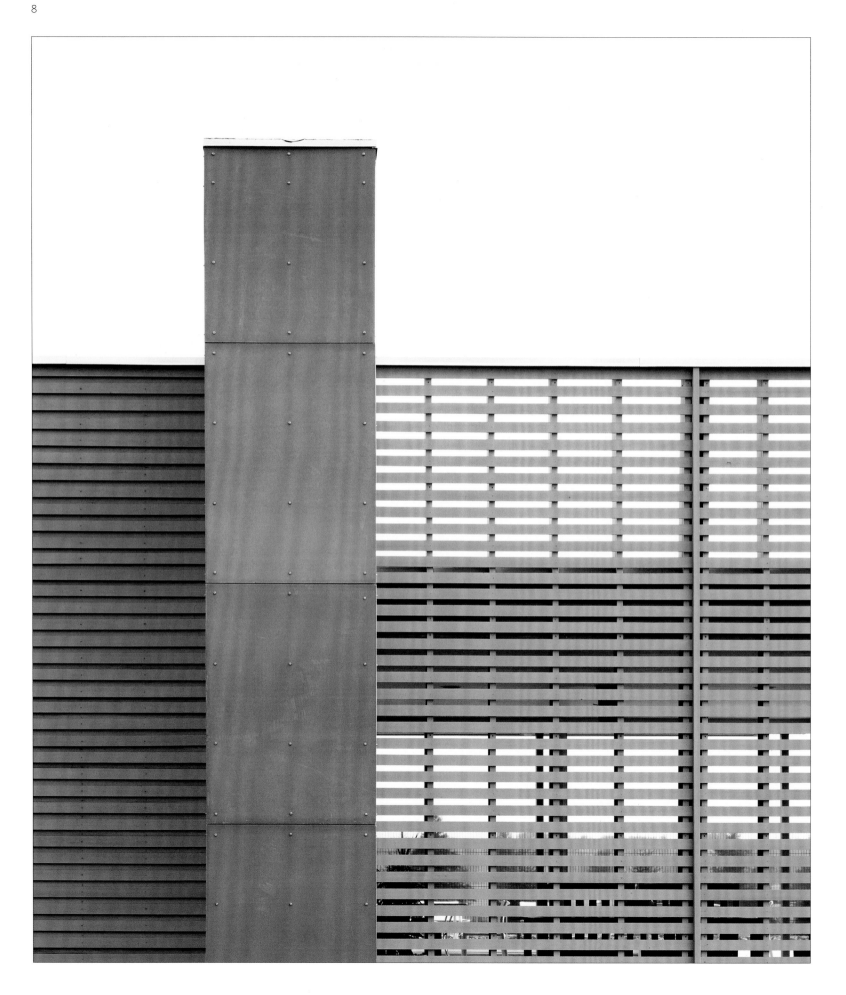

Look Close
Reed Kroloff

Earle Dickson and his industrious wife, Josephine, had a problem. In her many household projects, Josephine often cut or burned her fingers, and the bandages she fashioned wouldn't stay on. Earle improvised a solution by spacing blocks of gauze, overlaid with crinoline, at intervals along a roll of adhesive tape. Josephine would cut a strip of the tape and—voila—a quick and reliable bandage. Lucky for his employer, Johnson & Johnson, and lucky for us, Earle brought his idea to work in 1920. A grateful company made him vice president, and the world soon met the Band-Aid.

Band-Aids, Post-it Notes, credit cards—there are many seemingly modest products that disguise brilliant observation. To most, cellophane tape and cotton gauze are cellophane tape and cotton gauze. For Earle Dickson, they were more. For David Brininstool and Brad Lynch, they would be more.

Like that of Dickson, the success of Chicago's Brininstool + Lynch rests in its principals' ability to recognize potential where others might not, and then translate that capacity to the architectural scale. Watch, in these pages, as chalkboard erasers become conference rooms and corn cribs become houses. These transformations may not be magic in the classical sense—neither was Dickson's bandage—but it's something very few other architects can do, especially at this level of consistent invention.

With well over 200 projects completed, picking a favorite Brininstool + Lynch is a challenge: there are so many good ones, each with a distinct character. Yet there is an elegantly reductive logic that links the beautiful details and the simple forms, a clear language that is fresh and convincing. There is nothing self-conscious; nothing ill-considered. This architecture is controlled, yet rich in emotion and empathy. Like the work of Mies, a Brininstool + Lynch building is difficult to place in time, and like the work of Wright, it is impossible to separate it from its site. In this way, like those spiritual forebears, the office is very much of Chicago, its buildings at home anywhere.

This book explores twelve of the firm's projects for what they are: elegant ideas given physical form by gifted designers (working with visionary clients). These ideas range in scale and vary in location and cost. But no matter the scope, Brininstool + Lynch brings the same focused intensity to each. And with each, simple ideas become something profound.

Reed Kroloff is a principal at jones|kroloff and a nationally known commentator on architecture and urban design. He has served as director of the Cranbrook Academy of Art and Art Museum, dean of architecture at Tulane University, and editor-in-chief of *Architecture* magazine. In 2003, he received the Rome Prize from the American Academy in Rome.

Racine Art Museum
Racine, Wisconsin, 2003

The Racine Art Museum has its origins in a 1938 bequest from Jennie Wustum. For its first six decades, the institution was housed in Wustum's nineteenth-century residence to the northwest of the downtown area. By the 1990s, the museum had outgrown this location and decided to move the collection downtown.

The selected site is less than two blocks from Lake Michigan to the east and was occupied by the remnants of seven different structures, some dating back to the Civil War. The budget didn't permit creating an entirely new facility, so the task became one of turning the rough assemblage into a cohesive building suited to the needs of contemporary museum exhibition and administration. The old buildings were built as independent structures, so there was no uniformity between floor levels, window sizes, and the like. Most floor plates were demolished; the remaining few were entirely reconstructed, as were the interior spaces, to create new galleries.

The only way to achieve any kind of unity on the exterior was to reclad the building. Acrylic panels mounted horizontally in an aluminum truss system offer a consistency to the facade in an economical manner. What was left of the original building fronts hides behind the panels.

The primary entrance is on Main Street, emphasizing the central quality of the new location. The exterior of the first floor is wrapped in clear glass, which opens a view all the way through the museum. Inside, different ceiling heights and an expanse of translucent glass divide the first floor into zones. High ceilings and natural light signal the lobby and circulation. The translucent glass and lower ceilings demarcate an exhibition area. Between the translucent wall and the clear glass exterior wall is a place where non-light-sensitive objects can be displayed, as if in a retail storefront, encouraging passersby to enter the institution.

Simple means are used to create complex spaces within the museum. Liquid vinyl poured over a substrate of recycled rubber tires creates a smooth and resilient floor. White-painted wall planes articulate forms that respond to natural and artificial light, fostering an interplay of light and dark. A system of skylights and laylights filters natural light so that a wide range of materials can be displayed.

Mechanical systems—air diffusers and returns, lighting, controls—are incorporated into slots in the ceiling and hidden behind signage panels so that they do not distract from the art and the experience. The exhibition furniture throughout the museum was developed specifically for the display of three-dimensional works of various sizes.

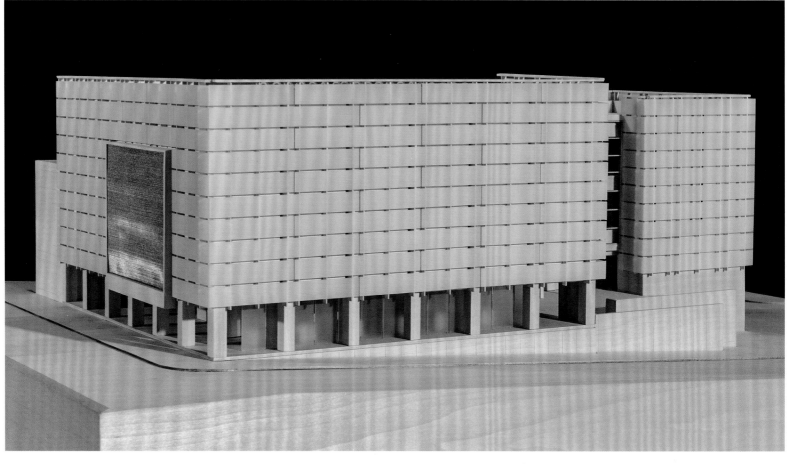

Racine Art Museum

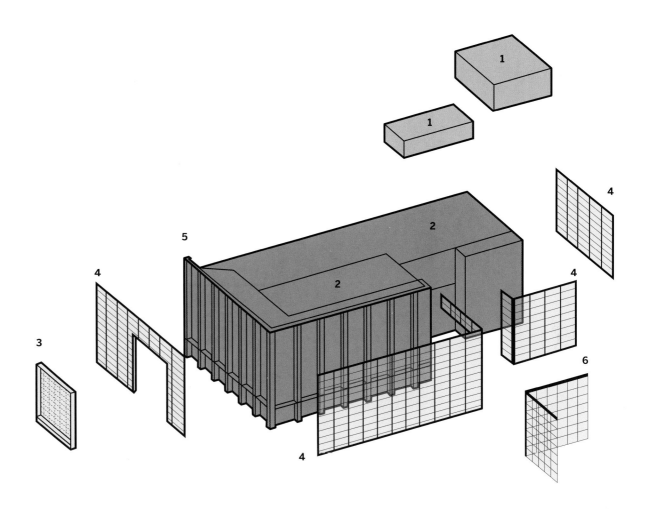

Exploded Axonometric

Existing Structure
1 Removal of Previous Additions
2 Remaining Building Structure

Applied Facade
3 Metal Screen
4 Acrylic Panels
5 Existing Masonry
6 Clear Glass

Cross Section

1 Gallery One
2 Gallery Two
3 Gallery Three
4 Lobby
5 Office
6 Storage

Long Section

1 Entry
2 Storage
3 Office

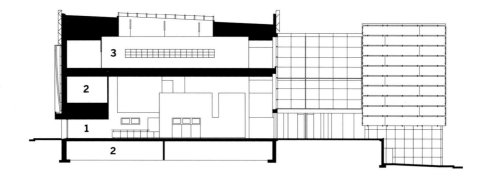

Third Floor Plan

1 Office
2 Conference
3 Kitchen
4 Open to Below

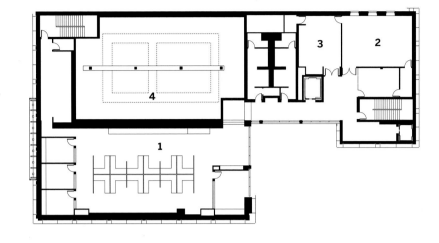

Second Floor Plan

1 Gallery Three
2 Library
3 Storage

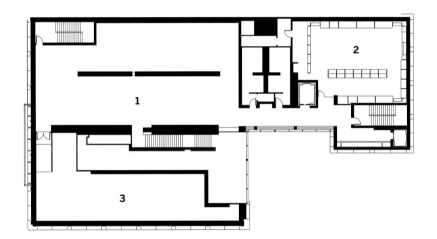

Ground Floor Plan

1 Entry
2 Gallery One
3 Museum Store
4 Gallery Two
5 Art Prep Area
6 Courtyard

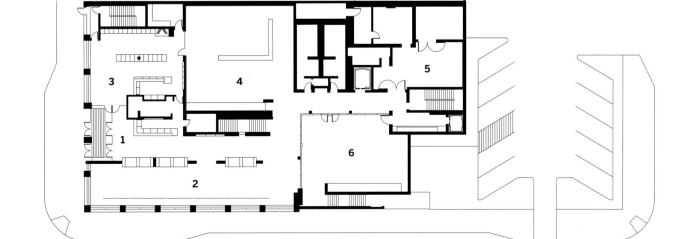

0   8 ft

Claremont House

Chicago, Illinois, 2007

Chicago is a neighborhood of front porches. Even the inhabitants of grand Prairie Avenue mansions socialized with neighbors from their stoops. The large window of this single-family house is an abstraction of the porch, an open engagement with the neighborhood.

The brick volume is not a monolithic shell but rather a composition of planes. Small limestone segments between the brick surfaces emphasize their planar quality.

The main entry is poised a half-level above the ground floor and a half-level below the main floor. The interior is organized into a logical progression, with a millwork volume containing most of the functional spaces: storage, food preparation, even a small powder room.

Both the stair and the wood volume align precisely with the smaller windows that are part of the primary facade. The openness of the stair, in conjunction with the operable windows, facilitates a turbinelike cooling effect.

Living, dining, and kitchen areas occupy the main floor. A small overlook, protected by a plane of translucent acrylic, gives a view a half-level down to the main entrance. Custom furniture, including a desk for the lower level and a sofa for the living area, is characterized by low profiles, open compositions, and slender structural framework.

A perforated metal box along one side of the back courtyard is essentially an extension of the millwork volume. This assemblage of zinc panels along with the brick wall below shields the courtyard from views from adjacent buildings.

The garage is a separate small volume at the rear of the site. Planted atop the garage are prairie grasses. The "crew cut" of the greenery is visible from the dining area on the main floor.

Third Floor/Roof Plan

1 Bedroom
2 Master Bedroom
3 Green Roof

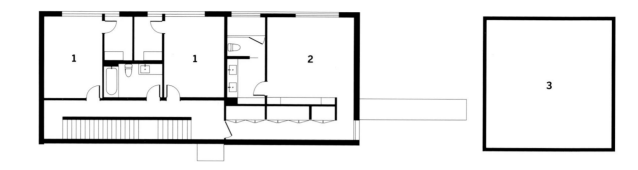

Second Floor Plan

1 Entry
2 Living
3 Dining/Kitchen
4 Courtyard
5 Garage

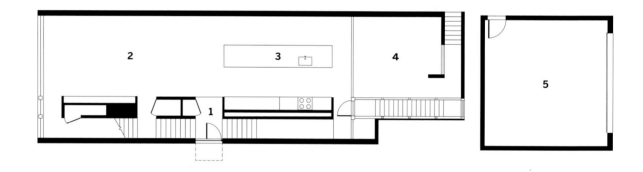

Ground Floor Plan

1 Guest Bedroom
2 Office/Family
3 Courtyard

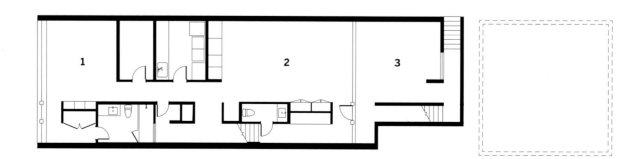

0   8 ft

Thermal Dynamics

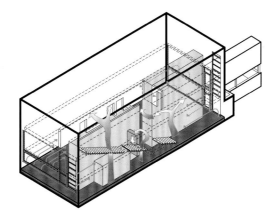 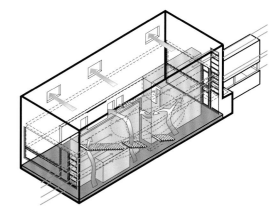

Radiant heat in the winter

Cool air circulation in the summer

Cross and Long Sections

1 Office/Family
2 Dining/Entry
3 Bedroom
4 Garage

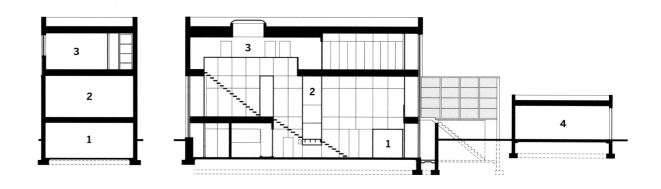

West and South Elevations

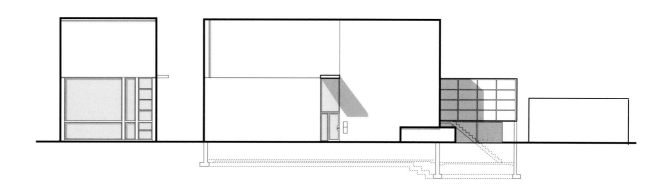

Coffou Cottage
Michigan City, Indiana, 2008

Many communities bordering Lake Michigan are densely developed along the water but less so just a few hundred yards inland. This weekend house is purposely set back from the road on a plot surrounded by protected meadows and woods, giving rise to a relative isolation unique in the area.

Inside, an expanse of glass opens the house to views of the woods. Opposite the main entry is a door to the meadow landscape. The route between the two portals forms an inglenook, a Prairie school trademark, here modernized with a fireplace surround of slate and a built-in sofa. Extending back from the sofa and defining one side of the living area is a wood volume that accommodates powder room, closets, laundry, and kitchen appliances. Clad in the red cedar of the house exterior, the millwork assembly expresses the inside-outside relationship characteristic of the entire building.

Indiana corn cribs alternate solid and open areas, allowing air to circulate around dried corn. Likewise, the board-and-batten screen indicating the living area transforms into slats at certain areas—roof parapet, screened porch, a single living room window—giving an inviting sneak preview of the activities within.

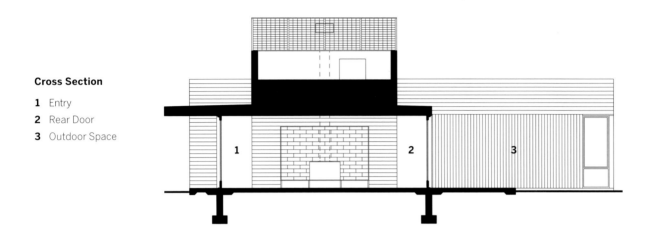

Cross Section

1 Entry

2 Rear Door

3 Outdoor Space

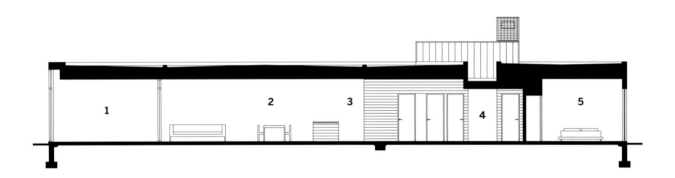

Long Section

1 Porch

2 Living/Dining

3 Kitchen

4 Hall

5 Bedroom

Floor Plan

1 Porch
2 Living/Dining
3 Kitchen
4 Pantry
5 Inglenook
6 Master Bedroom
7 Bedroom

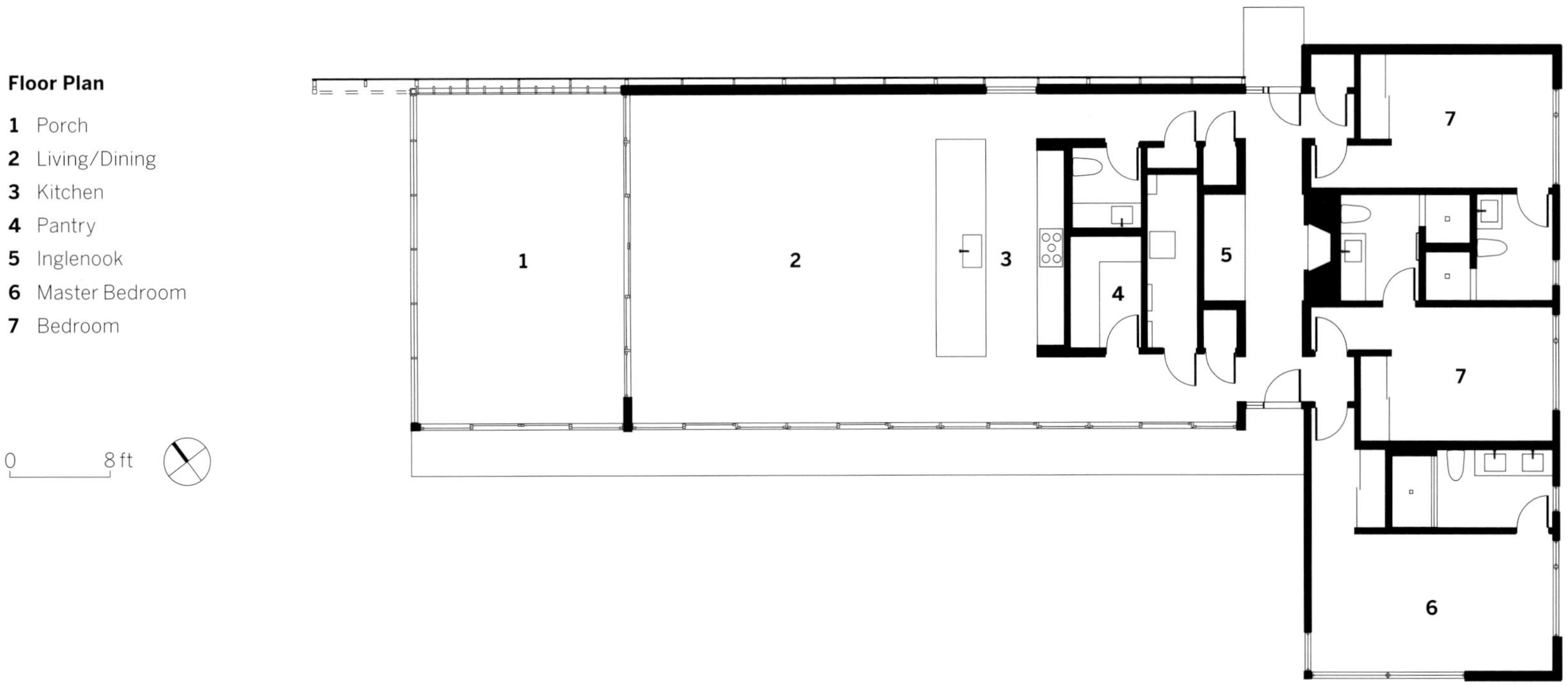

0   8 ft

Meyer Residence

Morris, Illinois, 2008

Many country houses for Chicagoans are sited along the shores of Lake Michigan, whether in Wisconsin, Illinois, Indiana, or Michigan. The clients for this year-round residence instead chose a large parcel—more than thirty acres—in a rural environment where they could relish outdoor life, breaking their own paths and opening their own views through the landscape.

The material palette interprets local agrarian structures—silos, barns, corn cribs—in a modern way and also nods to the tactile: corrugated zinc, board-formed concrete, and stacked wood. The T-shaped plan places the garage in one arm, a pool with a retractable roof in the other arm, and family areas in the stem. A long window set into the corrugated metal facade overlooking the outdoor courtyard serves as a clerestory for the living/dining area and also admits natural light to the lower portion of an upper-level corridor through a balustrade.

A large board-formed-concrete chimney volume demarcates one end of the living/ dining area. Although the house is large with generous interior spaces, it is energy efficient. Geothermal heating and cooling and passive means reduces operating costs.

It is essential to separate the humid environment of an indoor pool from the drier environment of living quarters; if not, the moist air can wreak havoc on artwork and interior finishes. The chimney volume limits the connection between spaces to a narrow passage, itself isolated by a glass vestibule.

Cross Section

1 Living/Dining
2 Kitchen
3 Mudroom
4 Bedroom
5 Storage

Long Section

1 Living/Dining
2 Stairs
3 Closet
4 Master Bedroom
5 Pool Area
6 Playroom
7 Music Room
8 Family Room
9 Storage
10 Mechanical

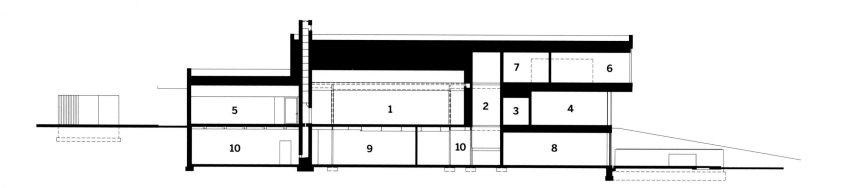

Meyer Residence

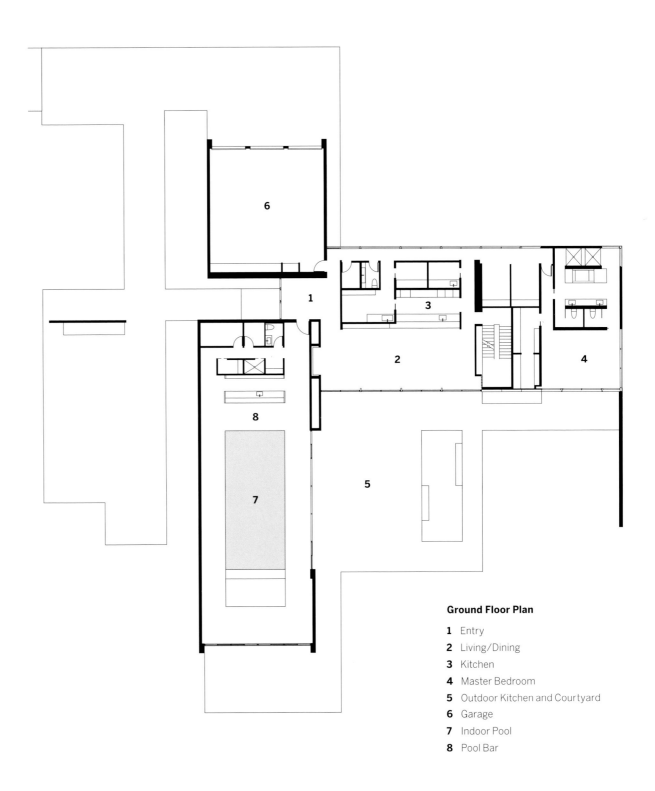

Ground Floor Plan

1 Entry
2 Living/Dining
3 Kitchen
4 Master Bedroom
5 Outdoor Kitchen and Courtyard
6 Garage
7 Indoor Pool
8 Pool Bar

0   8 ft

550 St. Clair

Chicago, Illinois, 2008

550 St. Clair occupies a prominent position three blocks west of Lake Shore Drive, one block east of Michigan Avenue, and just north of the Chicago River. The sides of the building facing Ohio Street, St. Clair Street, and Grand Avenue consist of taut planes of glass; the fourth side, which looks west over a three-story commercial structure fronting on Michigan Avenue, is marked by continuous horizontal balconies.

A six-story podium at the base of the building accommodates parking. The podium is sheathed in two layers of metal wall panels—a solid inner layer and a perforated outer layer. At night, lighting outlining the panels makes the base appear to float.

The primary entrance is oriented toward the pedestrian. Residents and visitors pass from the outdoor space (sidewalk) to outdoor/indoor space ("arcade" under the building overhang) to indoor/outdoor space (interior garden) to indoor space (lobby). The transitional space is accentuated with bright lighting.

The lobby is characterized by an interplay among exposed concrete, wood, terrazzo, stone, and glass. These materials both demarcate spaces and, as three-dimensional forms, occupy spaces. A corridor leading past the lobby desk takes a cue from Frank Lloyd Wright: the ceiling is compressed to exaggerate the double-height area of the lobby.

Condominium interiors adapt features more typically seen in single-family high-end residential. A soffit edging the exterior enclosure incorporates mechanical units, sprinkler lines, and lighting, all of which are usually exposed in living units. Interior walls are pulled back from the windows, bringing light to all interior spaces, easing the flow of interior circulation, and offering a generous perspective.

Corner balconies on the northeast and southeast corners highlight the floating quality of the clear glass facades at the north, east, and south. Accentuating this effect are the uppermost portions of the glass planes, which extend above the roof.

Typical Residential Floor Plan

1 Studio
2 One-Bedroom Unit
3 Two-Bedroom Unit
4 Three-Bedroom Unit

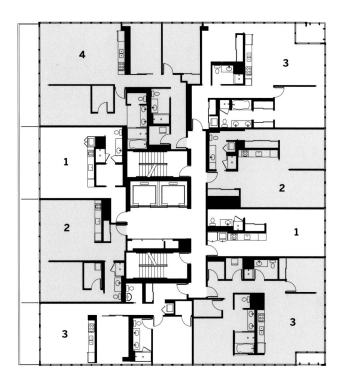

Ground Floor Plan

1 Residential Entry
2 Retail
3 Parking Ramp
4 Mechanical

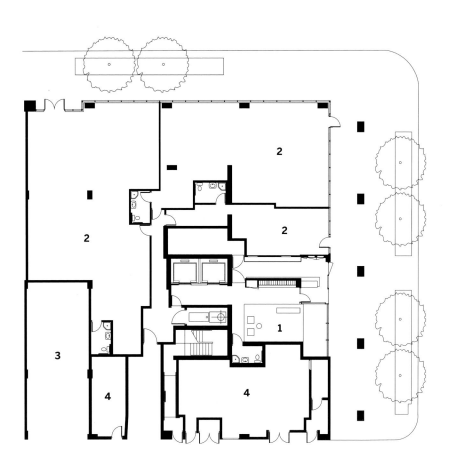

0   8 ft

Basecamp
Chicago, Illinois, 2010

The founders of Basecamp have dedicated themselves to improving the office experience, whether through the web-based project management software they have developed, a commitment to a calm professional culture, or the work environment itself. Among the objectives for their office, located in a loft space in a concrete building in the West Loop, were natural light throughout, or the perception of natural light; places where meetings or gatherings could take place without disturbing others; and a quiet and peaceful but still open workplace.

Whiteboards and their squeaky pens were discarded in favor of tactile and evocative chalkboards throughout the office. In many places, large planes of chalkboard are used instead of more conventional surfacing materials.

Accompanying the chalkboards are, of course, erasers. In addition to contributing an attractive, craftlike quality, heavy felt absorbs sound. Many interior walls and the entire core are wrapped in layered felt. Different depths of felt were applied in a pattern that both absorbs and diffuses—almost erases—sound.

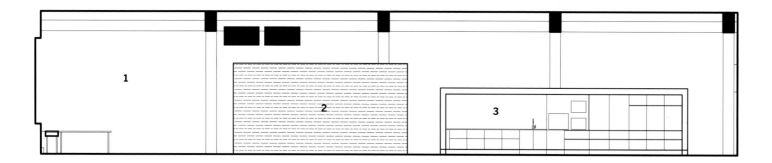

Interior Section/Elevation

1 Open Workroom

2 Printing/Services

3 Pantry/Coffee

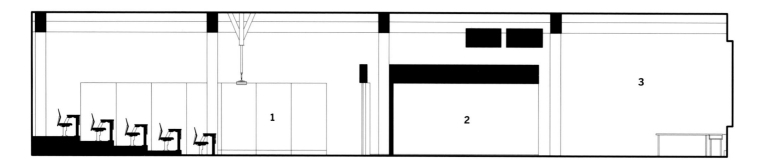

Interior Section/Elevation

1 Media Room

2 Team Room

3 Open Workroom

0 _____ 8 ft

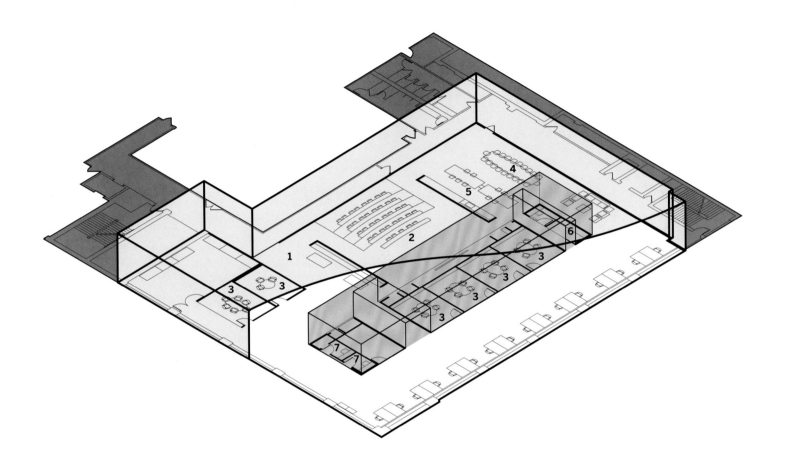

Axonometric

1 Reception/Library
2 Media Room
3 Team Room
4 Staff Dining
5 Pantry
6 Printing/Services
7 Phone Room

Coffou Apartment
Chicago, Illinois, 2010

Mies van der Rohe's four apartment towers along North Lake Shore Drive in Chicago, especially the original two at numbers 860 and 880, remain sought-after addresses for design aficionados even six decades after their completion.

The original plans are known for small bedrooms and bathrooms and inadequate kitchens, clearly designed by someone not recognized for his cookery. This apartment renovation retains a single bedroom, though it is separated by translucent glass rather than by a solid wall to make the apartment feel larger, and combines the small bathrooms into one generous space.

The apartment is large and open, offering striking views of Chicago and copious natural light. White millwork for storage and other functions almost disappears into the apartment envelope. The expansive new kitchen incorporates two more or less subtle homages to Mies: a substantial travertine table that references the lobby and entry plaza and—of course—MR chairs.

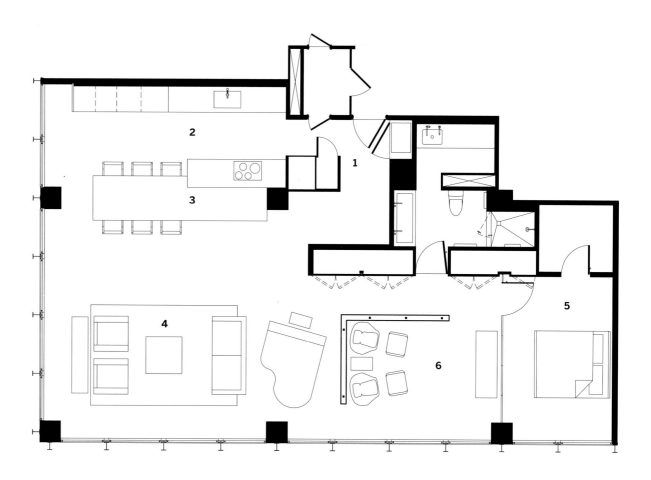

Floor Plan

0 ———————— 8 ft

1 Entry

2 Kitchen

3 Dining

4 Living

5 Bedroom

6 Media Room

Blue Office
Chicago, Illinois, 2012

Most 1970s-era high-rises, whether in Chicago or elsewhere, were built before the advent of the open office. Rather, they were organized hierarchically, with executives and managers in windowed private offices around the perimeter of the floor and support staff in a windowless bullpen in the center. The Blue Office turns this outdated paradigm not upside down but sideways.

The plan of the office resembles a doughnut—a doughnut with a solid center. That center is the building core, which is sheathed in vibrant backlit blue plastic. Layers of translucent and clear glass define the band around the core. Work tables occupy the zone next to the windows on one long and one short side of the space. At the other short side are a kitchen and eating area.

The remaining long side of the office has no windows because it is directly against the neighboring building. Lining this side is a feature wall about 100 feet long. The wall consists of hundreds of parallel slices of fiberboard cut by computer to form a rippling, elemental composition.

Backlit and well insulated, the sliced wall creates an attractive micro-environment within the office. Staffers gravitated to workstations along the wall despite the absence of nearby windows.

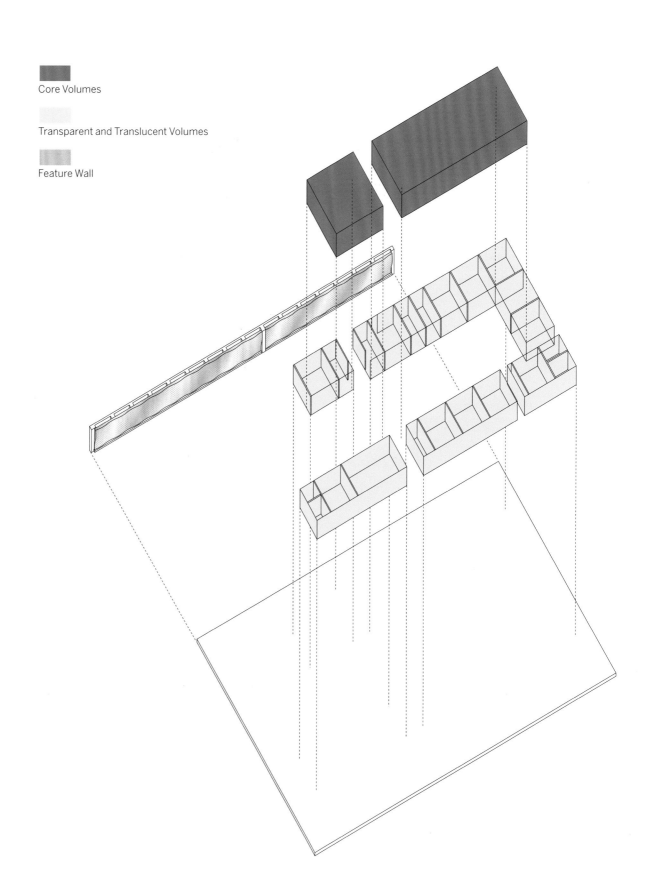

Core Volumes

Transparent and Translucent Volumes

Feature Wall

Fabrication Plans of Feature Wall

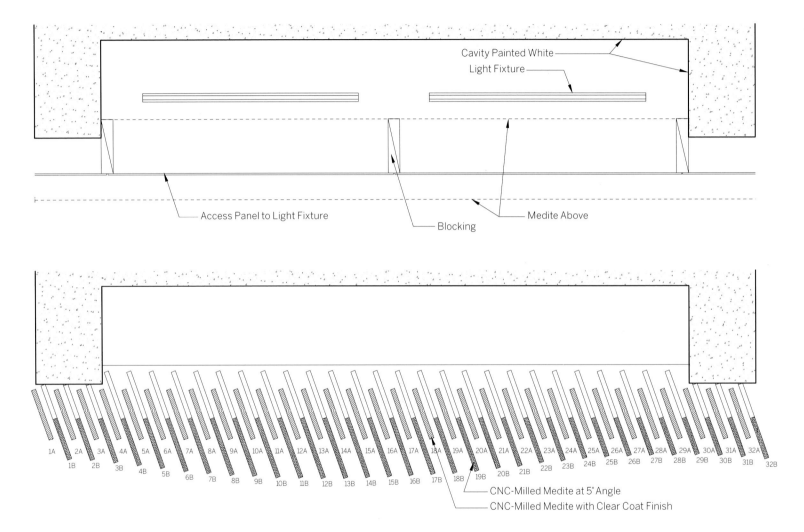

Cavity Painted White

Light Fixture

Access Panel to Light Fixture

Blocking

Medite Above

1A 2A 3A 4A 5A 6A 7A 8A 9A 10A 11A 12A 13A 14A 15A 16A 17A 18A 19A 20A 21A 22A 23A 24A 25A 26A 27A 28A 29A 30A 31A 32A

1B 2B 3B 4B 5B 6B 7B 8B 9B 10B 11B 12B 13B 14B 15B 16B 17B 18B 19B 20B 21B 22B 23B 24B 25B 26B 27B 28B 29B 30B 31B 32B

CNC-Milled Medite at 5° Angle

CNC-Milled Medite with Clear Coat Finish

0   1 ft

Section Through Feature Wall

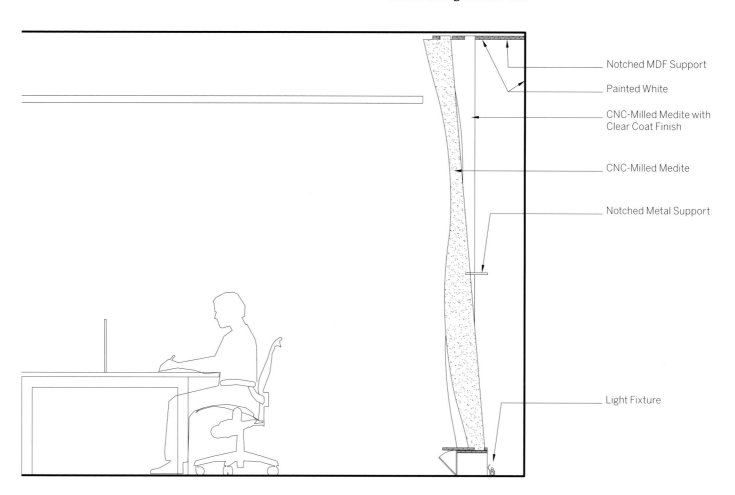

Notched MDF Support

Painted White

CNC-Milled Medite with
Clear Coat Finish

CNC-Milled Medite

Notched Metal Support

Light Fixture

Podesta Residence
Vero Beach, Florida, 2013

What is a modern architect to do when presented with a building site in a decidedly non-modern setting? The answer here was to follow the design guidelines, which called for an Anglo-Caribbean style, on the exterior, especially for the second level (peaked roofs, canted outdoor fireplace). By contrast, the interior and the courtyard landscape hold fast to modern attributes.

Indoors and outdoors are interwoven on the first floor (the main living level), as epitomized by two bodies of water. A reflecting pool—exactly the same length as the swimming pool and exactly the same width as the second-floor overhang—runs parallel to the primary exterior and interior walkways. The reflecting pool comes right up to the glass wall of the living/dining area, again emphasizing the indoor-outdoor relationship.

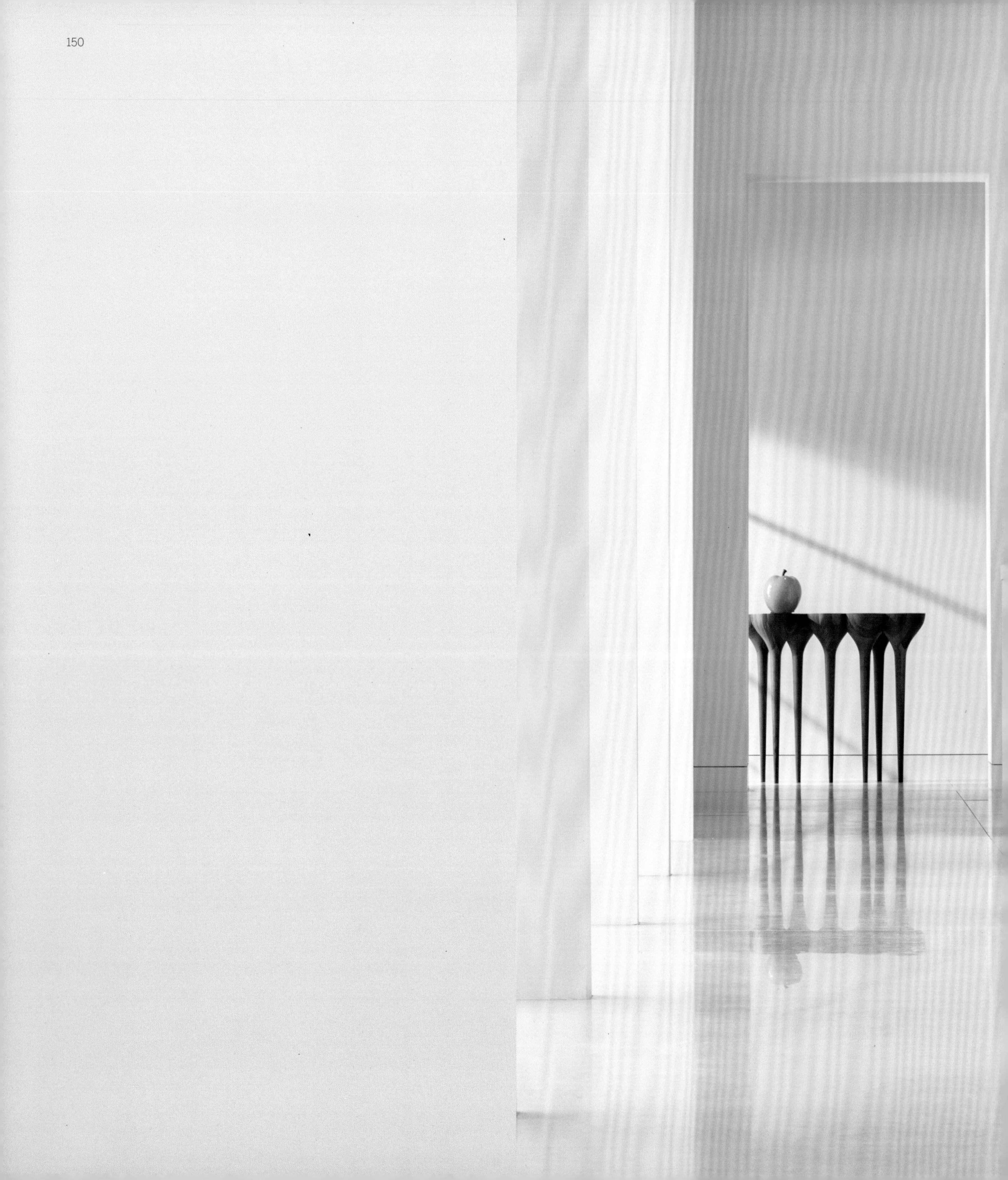

Two millwork volumes partition the first floor. Both present flat surfaces to the living space, suggesting a formal environment, and useful functions to the flanking areas: bookshelves and filing cabinets for the office; appliances and storage for the kitchen.

Podesta Residence

Meticulous detailing distinguishes all aspects of the house. The floor on the first level, both inside and outside, consists of large continuous limestone slabs, while the floor on the second level is composed of wide, dark-stained wood planks. The scissor stair picks up the same wood for handrails and floating treads. Hidden in thin slots where the walls meet the ceiling are mechanical diffusers and picture rail.

Ground Floor Plan

1 Entry
2 Courtyard
3 Pool
4 Reflecting Pool
5 Living
6 Dining
7 Kitchen
8 Garage
9 Utility
10 Office
11 Media Room

0   8 ft

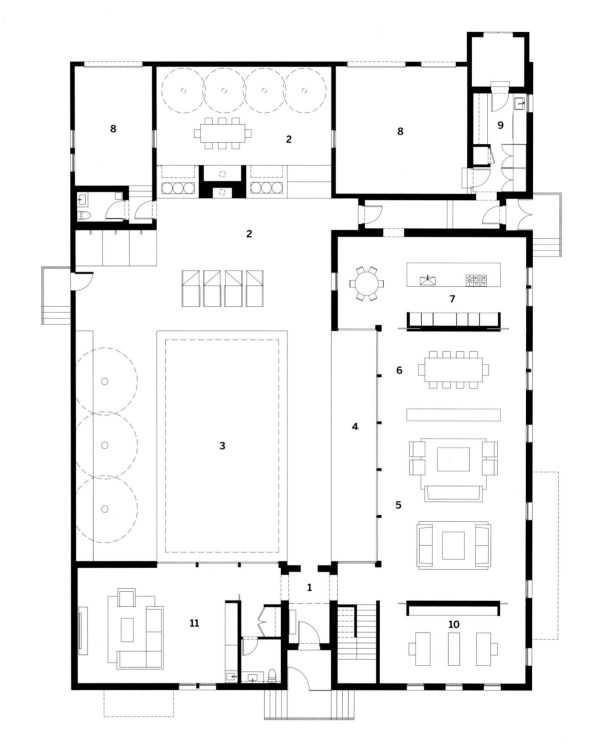

Wood House
Chicago, Illinois, 2013

The Wood House was named not for its client or for the common building material but for its location. Indeed, primary exterior materials are brick, steel, copper, and granite. The configuration of the house—a private indoor/outdoor sanctuary—was derived from the idea of a house volume situated within a larger volume.

The residence is focused around an interior courtyard. Large windows offer views from all angles. By contrast, the house presents a screened but not opaque aspect to the perimeter. The 8700-square-foot lot is three and a half feet below grade, a simple half-level shift that obstructs direct sightlines into the first and second floors of the house. Further shielding the house from the street is a Corten steel fence; the slats admit light to the front of the building but allow only oblique views in.

The materials of the house extend from inside to outside and outside to inside; they are treated similarly no matter the application. Steel-framed windows establish interior and exterior spaces with the most minimal of means. The L-shaped plan of the house accommodates the main living space in one section and all other functions in the second section. At the intersection between them is the entry, on the first floor, and the master bedroom, on the second floor. The main living space is sixteen feet high and topped by a laylight that admits both natural and artificial light. Mechanical diffusers, lighting, and switches are detailed so carefully that they disappear.

Three wood "boxes" inserted into the ground floor of the three-story section accommodate family functions. The first box incorporates the dining area, which was envisaged as a booth rather than a room, with intimate seating and low lighting, while the opposite side faces the entry and provides concealed storage and a powder room. The second box encloses the kitchen, with appliances and storage to either side. Between the second box and the third is the media room, which can be closed off by pocket doors extending from the boxes, and inside the third are the mud room, staircase, laundry room, and additional storage.

Wood House

A patinated copper screen patterned and perforated with dimples, debossing, and open squares protects the entry and the master bedroom from views from the street. The screen is more solid at the bottom and more open at the top.

The interior courtyard, which includes a kitchen, is used for outdoor dining and other activities. A planted pyramid divides the court and gives a sense of depth to the outdoor space.

Third Floor/Roof Plan

1 Studio
2 Guest Suite
3 Green Roof
4 Roof Deck

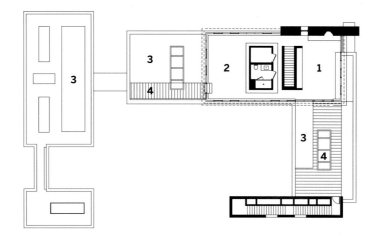

Second Floor Plan

1 Master Bedroom
2 Master Bath
3 Open to Below
4 Bedroom

Ground Floor Plan

1 Entry
2 Living
3 Dining
4 Kitchen
5 Media
6 Laundry
7 Mud Room
8 Outdoor Dining

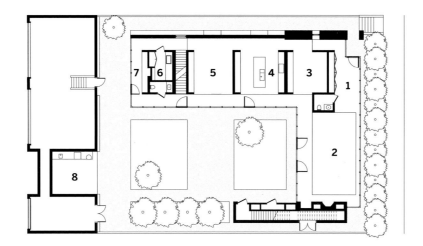

0   8 ft

Wood House

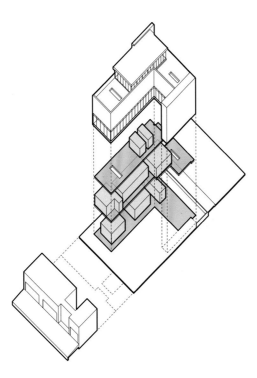

Core Volumes

- Millwork Volumes
- Floor Slabs

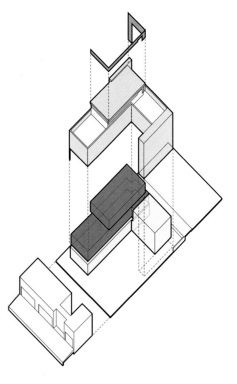

Private and Public

- Private Zone
- Public Zone
- Copper Privacy Screen

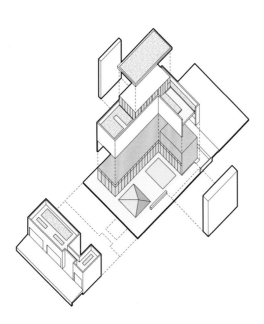

Green Roofs and Courtyard

- Green Roof
- Occupiable Outdoor Space
- Rooftop Garden

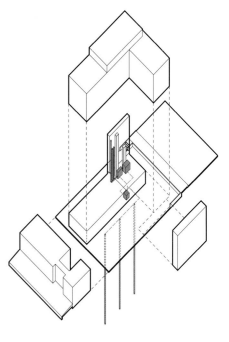

Geothermal and Mechanical Systems

- Return Air
- Supply Air
- - - Geothermal Supply

1345 South Wabash

Chicago, Illinois, 2015

This residential building is the first of two on neighboring sites in Chicago's South Loop. Between the two is a 65-foot-wide elevated garden; both buildings face this open green space, sharing the views and the light. 1345 South Wabash was the first condominium to be built in Chicago after the financial crisis of 2007–8, so the design was sensitive not only to aesthetics but to economy.

The lobby is just nine feet wide. The form liners required for any casting of concrete were modeled to produce the textured walls, merging structure and aesthetic. The elevators are set into a floating white plane, and the light fixtures are installed around the elevator doors and in the porcelain-tile floor. Exposed concrete ceilings and columns express the structure of the building within the apartments. The rooms open toward the windows, increasing the perceived size of the residential units.

To the south, the building abuts an older structure. Most residential buildings have double-loaded corridors, but here fire stairs and a single-loaded corridor run along the windowless south wall. The opposite facade, which faces north and looks over the garden, features a series of concrete balconies wrapped in perforated metal.

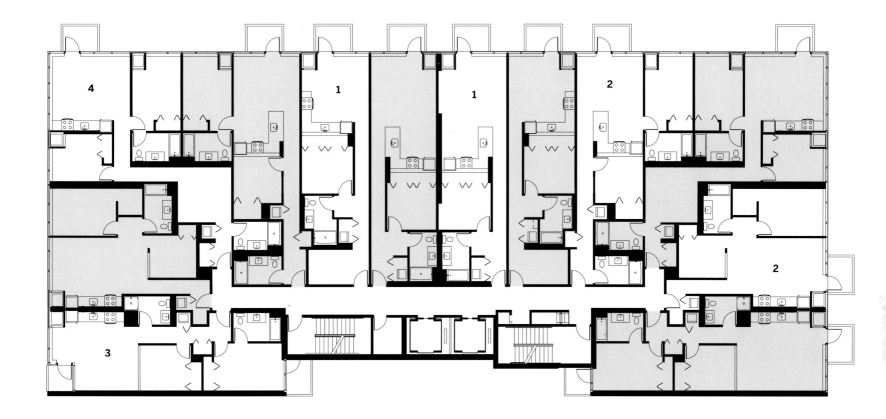

Typical Residential Floor Plan   0 ___ 8 ft

1 Junior One-Bedroom Unit
2 Junior Two-Bedroom Unit
3 Two-Bedroom Unit
4 Two-Bedroom plus Den Unit

710 West Grand
Chicago, Illinois, 2018

The Kennedy Expressway crosses the Northwest commuter line just a short distance from the River West site for this apartment building. The railway dictated the pointed form of the site. A conventional bar building was not the best use of the property; a better solution was to split a bar building into two parts, then relink them at an angle that echoed the site boundary.

Two kinds of glass—clear and opaque—ripple across the almost mirror-image main facades. A band of horizontal cement panels frames each of the faces, expressing the identity of the building. The white modular planks respond to the historic brick context of the active urban setting.

Angled walls define the modest entry, drawing residents and guests into the building. The horizontal cement planks lining the lobby are the same as those on the main facades, easing the transition between exterior and interior.

710 West Grand

Concept Diagram: Development of Split Bar

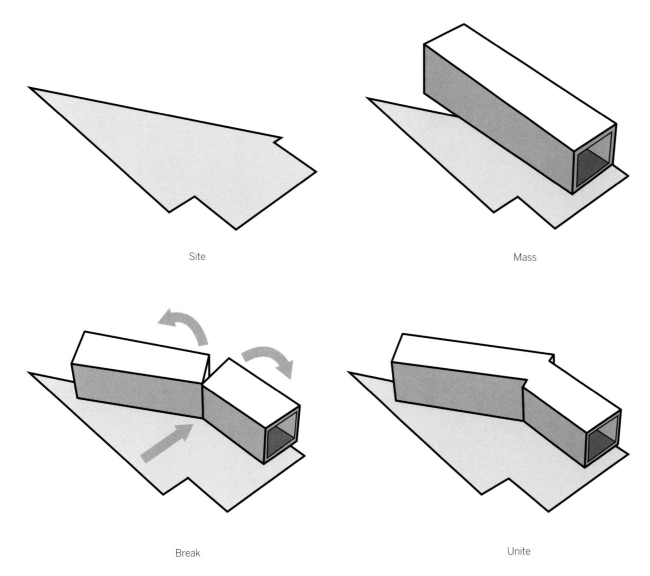

Site

Mass

Break

Unite

Site Plan with Ground Floor Plan

1 Residential Entry
2 Retail
3 Bicycle Room
4 Parking
5 Mechanical

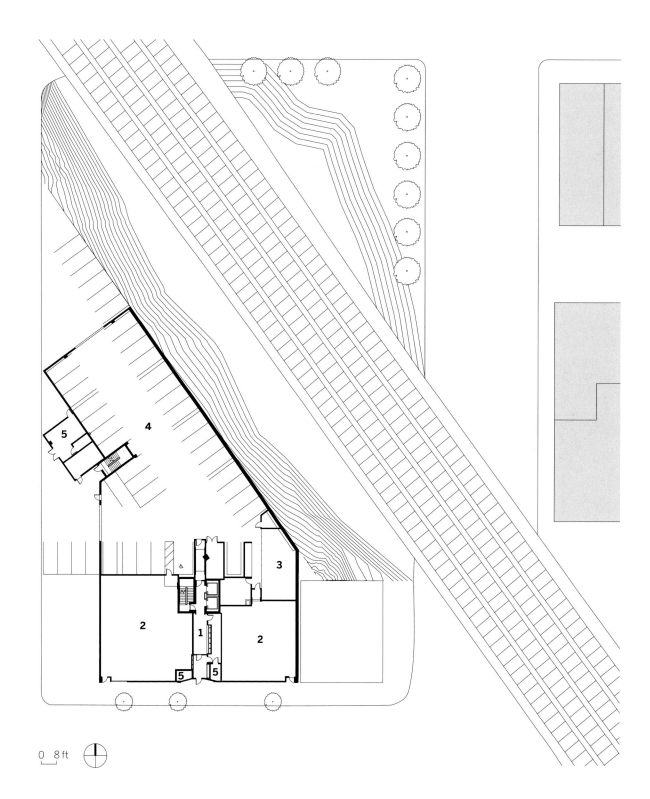

0 8 ft

Project Credits

Racine Art Museum, Racine, Wisconsin, 2003
Client Racine Art Museum Association
Photography Christopher Barrett, Hedrich Blessing
Contractor Bukacek Construction, Inc.
Partners Arnold & O'Sheridan Inc., structural, MEP;
Liska + Associates Inc., graphics and wayfinding
Team Brad Lynch, David Brininstool, Daniel Martus, Pablo Diaz,
Christine Marsal Brandl, Joanna Dabek Szymanska

Claremont House, Chicago, Illinois, 2007
Client Brad and Karen Lynch
Photography Christopher Barrett, Hedrich Blessing
Contractor Goldberg General Contracting, Inc.
Partner C. E. Anderson & Associates, structural
Team Brad Lynch, Lori Day

Coffou Cottage, Michigan City, Indiana, 2008
Client Jim and Sara Coffou
Photography Christopher Barrett, Hedrich Blessing
Contractor Mulcahy Builders
Partner C. E. Anderson & Associates, structural
Team Brad Lynch, Lori Day, Kevin Southard

Meyer Residence, Morris, Illinois, 2008
Client Raymond and Julieta Meyer
Photography Christopher Barrett, Hedrich Blessing
Contractor Vissering Construction Company
Partner C. E. Anderson & Associates, structural
Team Brad Lynch, Kevin Southard, Lori Day

550 St. Clair, Chicago, Illinois, 2008
Client Sutherland Pearsall
Photography Darris Lee Harris
Contractor Linn-Mathes, Inc.
Partners Terra Engineering, civil; C. E. Anderson &
Associates, structural; WCW Engineers Inc.,
mechanical; Environmental Group, electrical
Team David Brininstool, Daniel Martus,
Joanna Dabek Szymanska

Basecamp, Chicago, Illinois, 2010
Client Basecamp
Photography Christopher Barrett
Contractor Goldberg General Contracting, Inc.
Partners JB Engineering Services, LLC, electrical and
plumbing; Air-Rite Heating & Cooling, mechanical;
Stay Straight Manufacturing, millwork
Team Brad Lynch, Pablo Diaz, Dena Wangberg

Coffou Apartment, Chicago, Illinois, 2010
Client Jim and Sara Coffou
Photography Christopher Barrett
Contractor Goldberg General Contracting, Inc.
Partner WCW Engineers, Inc., MEP
Team Brad Lynch, Pablo Diaz, Dena Wangberg

Blue Office, Chicago, Illinois, 2012

Photography	Christopher Barrett
Contractor	Bear Construction
Partners	McGuire Engineers, MEP; Arup, acoustical
Team	Brad Lynch, Pablo Diaz

Podesta Residence, Vero Beach, Florida, 2013

Client	Juan and Alejandra Podesta
Photography	Christopher Barrett Photographer
Contractor	Huryn Construction
Partner	McCarthy and Associates, Inc., structural
Team	Brad Lynch, Daniel Martus, Kristen Padavic, Dena Wangberg

Wood House, Chicago, Illinois, 2013

Photography	Christopher Barrett Photographer
Contractor	Goldberg General Contracting, Inc.
Partners	Coen + Partners, landscape architecture; Goodfriend Magruder Structure LLC, structural; AA Service Company, mechanical; Moshe Calamaro & Associates, Inc., civil
Team	Brad Lynch, Daniel Martus, Dena Wangberg, Joice Krysak, Hillary Hyson, Eirik Agustsson

1345 South Wabash, Chicago, Illinois, 2015

Client	CMK Companies
Photography	Darris Lee Harris
Contractor	Lend Lease
Partners	C. E. Anderson & Associates, structural; Cosentini Associates, MEPFP; Eriksson Engineering, civil
Team	David Brininstool, Daniel Martus, Angelika Bukowska Zabiegala

710 West Grand, Chicago, Illinois, 2018

Client	ODG WPA LLC
Photography	Tom Rossiter
Contractor	ARCO/Murray
Partners	Eriksson Engineering, civil; Matson Ford, structural; WT Engineering, MEP
Team	David Brininstool, Daniel Martus, Angelika Bukowska Zabiegala, Jeremiah DeMoss

Additional Photography

Jacket Front	Christopher Barrett, Hedrich Blessing
Jacket Back	Christopher Barrett Photographer
Page 6	John Back
Page 8	Christopher Barrett, Hedrich Blessing
Page 28	Jon Bolton

Brininstool + Lynch

Midwestern natives David Brininstool and Brad Lynch founded Chicago-based Brininstool + Lynch in 1989. In the thirty years since, they have completed more than 250 buildings, across scales (single-family homes to high-rises) and landscapes (urban, suburban, and rural). In addition, the firm has been recognized with more than fifty major design awards, including twenty-eight AIA Design Excellence Awards. Both partners are fully engaged throughout the life of each project, collaborating with clients, consultants, and community and government entities.

Brininstool and Lynch have eight decades of shared and individual expertise. They met in the 1980s in the Chicago office Pappageorge Haymes. Previously, Brininstool studied architecture at the University of Michigan and worked at Skidmore, Owings & Merrill. Lynch was educated at the University of Wisconsin and worked as a construction and project manager on the restoration of several Frank Lloyd Wright structures, including the first Herbert Jacobs House, Wright's first Usonian House and a National Historic Landmark.

The partners are dedicated to improving society through the creation and promotion of design excellence. Brininstool and Lynch have been involved in civic, professional, and academic endeavors—locally, nationally, and internationally—throughout their careers. These activities, from investigation of advanced building techniques to engagement with professionals and laypersons who share their humanistic goals for architecture, inform and enhance the built work.

Office, 1989–2019

Eirik Agustsson
Tom Bassett-Dilley
Nicole Bauza
Jamie Berg
Camille Bernsten
Zubair Bhiadani
Camille Bivens
Sara Buhl Bjelke
Andre Boudreau
Christine Marsal Brandl
Marissa Brown
Seely Brunstrom
Mollie Buhrt
Javier Buscaglia-Pesquera
Troy Carlson
Yunji Chung
Nick Custer
Nandin Erdene Dashondog
Lori Day
Mare DeCampos
Jeremiah DeMoss
Thomas Denney
Pablo Diaz
Sandra Robison Dold
Lee Donghyun
Matthew Ehrhard
Cheryl Elsbury
Mary English
Ellen Evangelides
Carrie Evans
Bill Foelmer
Brian Foster
Brad Fowler
Joseph Gamblin

Edouard Gillon
Keith Ginnodo
Trisha Girdwood
Veronica Gomez
Irene Paola Gomez-Pineiro
Lydia Gouveia
Xiao Gu
Jun Guo
Chooyon Han
Zia Hillocks
Hillary Hyson
S. Evans Jones
Callie Eitzen Kesel
Joice Krysak
Brian Kulezic
Somin Lee
Jason Longo
Blake Lynch
Anthony Manzo
Daniel Martus
Kristina Mayorchak
John McCarthy
George Merema
Kara Moeller
David Mulder
Maya Nash
Jacob Newton
Nguyen Nguyen
Olesegun Obasanjo
Susana Odriozola
Kristen Padavic
Mike Padavic
Jong Park
Dominic Passeri

Steve Poston
Jerico Prater
Sergio Preston
David Rariden
Matthew Reiskin
Mina Rezaeian
Stephen Salazar
Ashley Satterfield
Marcia Schilling
Matthew Scholl
Seema Scholl
Catie Schroeder
Dan Seagraves
Dolly Sehr
David Siepmann
Zev Solomon
Chelsia Sooksengdao
Kevin Southard
Mark Szostak
Joanna Dabek Szymanska
Ian Thomas
Jim True
Dena Wangberg
Brooks Wehner
Joe Weishaar
Daley Wilson
Joe Windler
Sarah Peil Winstead
Desiree Wong
Joshua Yoon
Jim Yoshida
Angelika Bukowska Zabiegala
Andrea Zaff
Thaddeus Zarse

Bold indicates current team.

Acknowledgments

There are few things as rewarding in architecture as working with a great client. Many of ours have become close friends that continue to challenge and encourage us. Without them, there would be no architecture for us to build. We thank them wholeheartedly.

We have been fortunate to have in our studio many talented architects, both in the past and currently. They have helped facilitate our common goals and visions. In particular, we recognize Pablo Diaz and Dan Martus; cumulatively, they have been the backbone of our firm for more than forty years.

Elizabeth Kubany, always a voice of calm and reason, introduced us to our editor and our publisher. Gianfranco Monacelli, Alan Rapp, and Michael Vagnetti of The Monacelli Press have been enthusiastic about this project from the outset.

This book could not have been realized without the patience and prodding of Andrea Monfried and Reed Kroloff. Reed has advised and encouraged us in our work for more than two decades, and Andrea brought many attributes and talents to this project. Our long-time friend and close collaborator Steve Liska has made us look good with his exceptional design—as always. We are grateful to all.

BL + DB